Believe · Celebrate · Live™

Eucharist

Preparing to Celebrate First Communion

The Subcommittee on the Catechism, United States Conference of Catholic Bishops, has found this text, copyright 2017, to be in conformity with the *Catechism of the Catholic Church*.

S®ᵈˡⁱᵉʳ Sadlier Religion

Believe • Celebrate • Live™
…developed by the community of faith through…

Catechetical and Liturgical Consultants
Carole M. Eipers, D.Min.
National Catechetical Advisor
William H. Sadlier, Inc.

Donna Eschenauer, Ph.D.
Associate Dean
Associate Professor, Pastoral Theology
St. Joseph's Seminary
Yonkers, NY

Matthew Halbach, Ph.D.
St. Joseph Educational Center
West Des Moines, IA

Tom Kendzia, B.Mus.Ed.
Composer and Director of Music
Christ the King Parish
Kingston, RI

Barbara Sutton, D.Min.
Associate Dean of Ministerial
    Formation and Outreach
St. John's School of Theology and Seminary
Collegeville, MN

Theological Consultants
Most Reverend Edward K. Braxton,
    Ph.D., S.T.D.
Official Theological Consultant
Bishop of Belleville

Monsignor John E. Pollard, S.T.L.
Pastor, Queen of All Saints Basilica
Chicago, IL

Reverend Donald Senior, CP, Ph.D., S.T.D.
Member, Pontifical Biblical Commission
President Emeritus of Catholic Theological
    Union
Chicago, IL

Inculturation Consultants
C. Vanessa White, Ph.D.
Catholic Theological Union
Chicago, IL

Dulce M. Jiménez-Abreu
Director of Bilingual Religion Markets
William H. Sadlier, Inc.

Luis J. Medina, M.A.
Bilingual Consultant
St. Louis, MO

Curriculum and Child Development Consultant
Thomas S. Quinlan, M.Div.
Director, Religious Education Office
Diocese of Joliet

Special Needs Consultants
Charleen Katra, M.A.
Associate Director Specializing in
    Disability Ministry
Archdiocese of Galveston-Houston

Madonna Wojtaszek-Healy, Ph.D.
Consultant for Special Needs, Religious
    Education Office
Diocese of Joliet

Media/Technology Consultant
Spirit Juice Studios
Chicago, IL

Sadlier Consulting Team
Suzan Larroquette
Director of Catechetical Consultant
    Services

Kathy Hendricks
National Catechetical Consultant

Timothy R. Regan
Regional Vice President

Writing/Development Team
Diane Lampitt, M.Ed.
Vice President, Product Management,
    Religion

Alexandra Rivas-Smith
Executive Vice President, Product
    Management

Mary Carol Kendzia
Research and Development Director,
    Religion

Joanne McDonald
Editorial Director

Regina Kelly
Supervising Editor

William M. Ippolito
Director of Corporate Planning

Editors
Ellen Marconi, Dignory Reina, Gloria
Shahin, Robert Vigneri

Publishing Operations Team
Blake Bergen
Vice President, Publications

Carole Uettwiller
Vice President of Planning and Technology

Robert Methven
Vice President, Digital Publisher

Vince Gallo
Senior Creative Director

Francesca O'Malley
Art/Design Director

Cesar Llacuna
Senior Image Manager

Cheryl Golding
Production Director

Monica Reece
Senior Production Manager

Jovito Pagkalinawan
Electronic Prepress Director

Martin Smith
Planning and Analysis Project Director

Yolanda Miley
Accounts and Permissions Director

Lucy Rotondi
Business Manager

Design/Image Staff
Kevin Butler, Nancy Figueiredo, Stephen Flanagan,
Lorraine Forte, Debrah Kaiser, Gabriel Ricci,
Bob Schatz, Karen Tully

Production Staff
Robin D'Amato, Carol Lin, Vincent McDonough,
Allison Pagkalinawan, Laura Reischour

Photo Credits
age fotostock/Andria Patino: 79 *right*; Tetra Images: 37, 63; Wavebreak Media: 23, 77. Corbis/Igor Emmerich: 51 *right*; ML Harris: 9 *right*; Masterfile/Laurie Rubin: 9 *left*. Dreamstime. com/Jennifer Pitiquen: 93. Neal Farris: 65. Fotolia/littleny: 9 *center*; orensila: 44 *bottom*. Getty Images/CE Futcher: 21; Image Source: 51 *left*; Jose Luis Pelaez: 35. Masterfile/Royalty-Free Division: 79 *left*, 84 *center left*; Radius Images: 84 *top*, 90 *bottom*. Valeta Orlando: 15 *left*, 20 *bottom*. Shutterstock.com/ankudi: 78 *bottom*; binik: 50 *bottom*; Denis Cristo: 46; deedl: 32; dvande: 94; foodonwhite: 74; Pagina: 60; PGMart: 16 *background*, 30 *background*, 44 *background*, 58 *background*, 72 *background*, 86 *background*; pgvector: 72 *bottom*; Pixejoo: 58 *bottom*; Ann Precious: 64 *bottom*; Yuliya Proskurina: 18; Nina Rys: 88; WDG Photo: 63 *background*. Spirit Juice Studios: 6, 7, 8, 12, 13, 14, 15 *right*, 16, 20 *top*, 22, 26, 27, 28, 29, 30, 34, 36, 40, 41, 42, 43, 44 *top*, 48, 50 *top*, 54, 55, 56, 57, 58 *top*, 62, 64 *top*, 68, 69, 70, 71, 72 *top*, 76, 78 *top*, 82, 84 *left*, 84 *center right*, 84 *right*, 85 *left*, 85 *right*, 86, 90 *top*, 91, 92. Getty Images/Jupiterimages: 49; Jamie Grill: 85 *center*.

Illustrator Credits
Robert Kayganich: 4-5. James Madsen: 10-11, 19, 24-25, 33, 38-39, 47, 52-53, 61, 66-67, 75, 80-81, 86 *center right*, 89. Phil Parks: 83. Zina Saunders: 17, 31, 45, 59, 73.

Nihil Obstat
Rev. Matthew S. Ernest, S.T.D.
Rev. Kevin J. O'Reilly, S.T.D.
Censores Librorum

Imprimatur
✠ His Eminence, Timothy Cardinal Dolan
Archbishop of New York
May 12, 2017

The *Nihil Obstat* and *Imprimatur* are official declarations that a book or pamphlet is free of doctrinal or moral error. No implication is contained therein that those who have granted the *Nihil Obstat* and *Imprimatur* agree with the contents, opinions, or statements expressed.

Acknowledgments
Excerpts from the English translation of *The Roman Missal* © 2010, International Committee on English in the Liturgy, Inc. (ICEL). All rights reserved.

Scripture excerpts are taken from the *New American Bible with Revised New Testament and Psalms*. Copyright © 1991, 1986, 1970, Confraternity of Christian Doctrine, Inc. Washington, D.C. Used with permission. All rights reserved. No part of the *New American Bible* may be reproduced by any means without permission in writing from the copyright owner.

Excerpts from the English translation of the *Catechism of the Catholic Church* for the United States of America, copyright © 1994, United States Catholic Conference, Inc.—Libreria Editrice Vaticana. English translation of the *Catechism of the Catholic Church: Modifications from the Editio Typica* copyright © 1997, United States Catholic Conference, Inc.—Libreria Editrice Vaticana. Used with permission.

Excerpts from the English translation of *Rite of Baptism for Children* © 1969, ICEL. All rights reserved.

Excerpts from *Catholic Household Blessings and Prayers (Revised Edition)* © 1988, 2007, United States Conference of Catholic Bishops, Washington, D.C. Used with permission. All rights reserved.

English translation of the Lord's Prayer and Apostles' Creed by the International Consultation on English Texts (ICET).

"Lead Us to the Water" Text © 1998, Tom Kendzia. Music © 1998, Tom Kendzia and Gary Daigle. Published by OCP, 5536 NE Hassalo, Portland, OR 97213. All rights reserved. "Rain Down" © 1991, Jaime Cortez. Published by OCP, 5536 NE Hassalo, Portland, OR 97213. All rights reserved. Used with permission. "Lord, Hear My Prayer" by Jim Gibson, Copyright © 2001 by GIA Publications, Inc., 7404 S. Mason Ave., Chicago, IL 60638 • www.giamusic.com • 800.442.1358. All rights reserved. Used by permission. "Oyenos, Señor" by Jim Gibson, tr. by Jaime Cortez, Copyright © 2001 by GIA Publications, Inc. All rights reserved. Used by permission. "Our God Is Here" © 2001, Chris Muglia. Published by Spirit & Song, a division of OCP. 5536 NE Hassalo, Portland, OR 97213. All rights reserved. Used with permission. "Pan de Vida" Text: John 13:1–15; Galatians 3:28–29; Bob Hurd and Pia Moriarty. Text and music © 1988, Bob Hurd and Pia Moriarty. Published by OCP. All rights reserved. "Somos el Cuerpo de Cristo" Text: Jaime Cortez and Bob Hurd. Text and music © 1994, Jaime Cortez. Published by OCP. All rights reserved.

Contents

1 sanctuary
2 altar
3 crucifix
4 tabernacle
5 sanctuary lamp
6 ambo
7 chalice
8 paten
9 cruets
10 presider's chair
11 processional cross
12 Paschal Candle
13 baptismal font or pool
14 Stations of the Cross
15 Reconciliation Room or confessional
16 stained glass
17 pews
18 statue of Mary

Welcome

This is a time of great joy for you and your family as you prepare to celebrate your First Holy Communion. There will be many people to guide you on your journey with Jesus. The whole parish community is praying for you during this special time in your life.

As you go through each chapter:

Believe

You will recognize God's presence in your life as you recall your stories and as you see and hear the Word of God in the Scripture stories.

Celebrate

You will learn about the Church's celebration of the Eucharist as you prepare to celebrate your First Holy Communion.

Live

You will respond to God's grace by continuing to grow as a disciple of Jesus Christ.

May you always recognize God's action and presence in your life!

Belonging to the Church

"The Christian community welcomes you with great joy."

—*Rite of Baptism*

Believe

Open Your Heart

Things I do with my family include . . .

_____

_____

_____

_____

_____

My family celebrates . . .

_____

_____

_____

_____

I show love for my family by . . .

_____

_____

_____

_____

Doors that Welcome

Each one of us is a son or daughter. We belong to a family. When we are baptized we become members of a larger family, the Church, the Body of Christ. We become sons and daughters of God.

What is it like to knock on a door and be welcomed inside?

Baptism is the doorway into the Church. Through this first sacrament God welcomes you into his family and into his house. The Church has welcomed babies, children, and adults of all ages through Baptism since the earliest times.

"Behold, I have left an open door before you, which no one can close."

 REVELATION 3:8

Believe

The Word of the Lord

Jesus told his disciples that he would return to his Father in heaven. But he said that the Holy Spirit would be with them to guide them. The Holy Spirit would help them remember everything that Jesus had said and done.

 Based on ACTS OF THE APOSTLES 2:1–4, 38–41

Jesus' first disciples and Mary, the Mother of Jesus, were gathered together in a room because they were afraid. Suddenly they heard a noise. It sounded like a strong wind. They saw what looked like a flame of fire over each one of them.

"And they were all filled with the holy Spirit." (Acts of the Apostles 2:4)

They left the room. Then Peter, one of Jesus' Apostles, began teaching. He also invited the people to be baptized. Peter said that they, too, would receive the Gift of the Holy Spirit.

"Those who accepted his message were baptized, and about three thousand persons were added that day."

(Acts of the Apostles 2:41)

Celebrate

The Church

To receive the salvation from sin that Christ offers us, we must be baptized. In Baptism, we become members of Christ and his Church. We die to sin and rise to new life in Christ. We become members of the Body of Christ and temples of the Holy Spirit, and we share in the priesthood of Christ. This is what Christ wants for us.

In Baptism, we become a part of the Catholic Church. The **Church** is the community of people who are baptized and are called to follow Jesus Christ. The Church is the Body of Christ. In the Church we learn and pray together.

As Catholics we believe in the **Blessed Trinity**. The Blessed Trinity is the Three Persons in One God: God the Father, God the Son, and God the Holy Spirit. We believe that Jesus Christ is the Son of God, the Second Person of the Blessed Trinity, who became man. He died and rose from the dead to save, or heal, us from our sins.

Parish communities gather to worship.

In the Church we are called to love God and others the way Jesus did. We can do this with the help of the Holy Spirit.

There are members of the Catholic Church all over the world. Catholics gather together as parish communities to worship God and to share and celebrate God's love, especially on Sundays. We gather to celebrate the Eucharist, also called the **Mass**, and the other sacraments. We gather to show our love for God and others. We show reverence, or honor and respect, to God. He is our Creator and Father who sent his only Son, Jesus Christ, to save us from sin and help us to live as God's children.

Celebrate

Sacraments of Christian Initiation

The **sacraments** are special signs given to us by Jesus through which we share in God's life and love. The Church celebrates Seven Sacraments. Every time the Church celebrates a sacrament, Jesus is with us through the power of the Holy Spirit. On earth Jesus shared his life with his disciples, through his words and actions. In the sacraments, he shares his life with us, his disciples today. God's life in us makes us holy. We call God's life in us grace. The gift of grace that we receive in the sacraments is **sanctifying grace**. Grace is also at work in our daily lives through **actual grace**.

The Sacraments of Baptism, Confirmation, and Eucharist are the foundation of our lives as Jesus' disciples. Baptism is the first sacrament we receive. Original Sin and any sins we have personally committed are taken away. We become children of God and members of the Church. At Baptism, the priest or deacon places us in water, which is blessed, or pours the water over our heads.

No one is ever too young or too old to receive new life in Christ. It is truly a gift, not something we earn.

The priest or deacon baptizes us in the name of the Father, the Son, and the Holy Spirit. He anoints us with oil, a sign of the Gift of the Holy Spirit we receive for the first time. In Confirmation, a bishop anoints us with oil. This shows we are sealed with the Gift of the Holy Spirit and strengthened to live as disciples of Jesus.

In the Sacrament of the Eucharist, the whole Church remembers Jesus' Death and Resurrection.

In Eastern Catholic Churches, the Sacraments of Christian Initiation are celebrated together: first Baptism, then Confirmation, then Eucharist. This practice shows the unity of these three sacraments.

When we receive Holy Communion, we receive the Body and Blood, soul and divinity, of Jesus Christ.

Confirmation seals us with the Gift of the Holy Spirit.

The Eucharist is the center of our life. In the Eucharist the bread and wine become the Body and Blood of Jesus Christ. We receive Jesus Christ himself in Holy Communion.

Live

Become What You Believe

I am a member of the Catholic Church.

The pope's name is _____.

I was baptized in _____ Parish.

Today I belong to _____ Parish.

Our pastor's name is _____.

What I like best about my parish is . . .

_____

_____

_____

What makes my parish special is . . .

_____

_____

_____

At Baptism, I became a disciple of Jesus and a member of the Church!

Discipleship in Action

Saint Dominic Savio (1842–1857)

Dominic Savio was named Domenico Savio at his Baptism. He lived in a village in Italy. His name means "belonging to God." Church leaders said Dominic was "small in size, but a towering giant in spirit." At home, he prayed and said grace at mealtime with his family. At school, he studied hard. Dominic always tried to do what was right. He stopped his friends from fighting and helped those in need. Whenever Dominic spoke about his First Holy Communion, he said with joy, "That was the happiest and most wonderful day of my life!"

As a disciple I can . . .

Live

Lead Us to the Water

Leader: Let us pray the Sign of the Cross and then sing together "Lead Us to the Water."

All: (*Sing*) Lead us to the water, bring us to the feast. Wash us in the river, and fill us with your peace.

Leader: Lord Jesus, we thank you for the gift of faith. It is you who calls us each by name to become your followers.

All: (*Sing*) Lead us to the water, bring us to the feast. Wash us in the river, and fill us with your peace.

Leader: Lord Jesus, we have heard your call to love one another. From the waters of Baptism we are sent to be your light in our homes and in the world.

All: (*Sing*) Lead us to the water, bring us to the feast. Wash us in the river, and fill us with your peace.

Leader: Come forward to bless yourselves with the holy water from the bowl. Let this water remind us of our Baptism, as we ask Jesus to help us to bring his light and peace to the world.

All: (*Sing*) Lead us to the water, bring us to the feast. Wash us in the river, and fill us with your peace.

Leader: Let us fold our hands and pray as Jesus taught us.

All: Our Father . . .

Living Faith at ome

Take a few minutes to reflect on the Scripture art. Ask God to open your eyes and your heart. What feelings do you experience? How does the image inspire you? How are you like Jesus' first disciples? What else do you see? Pray a silent prayer of gratitude.

"And they were all filled with the holy Spirit."

✝ ACTS OF THE APOSTLES 2:4

Growing in Fai†h Together

Help your child to appreciate and treasure the blessings of the Catholic faith that you are passing on. Look at each faith message below. Share from your heart, and listen for the beauty and truth your child holds. Take some quality time together.

We become disciples of Jesus through Baptism, the doorway into the Church. God embraces us as his children. The Christian community welcomes us as members of the Church.

✝ Talk with your child about why you wanted him or her to be a member of the Church. Look at photographs and share memories of your child's Baptism, including the people who joined in the celebration of the sacrament.

We become full members of the Church through the Sacraments of Christian Initiation—Baptism, Confirmation, and the Eucharist. God fills us with his grace—his own life within us! We continue to grow as disciples of Jesus Christ.

✝ Recognize God's presence within your child. Give examples of your child's kind, welcoming, or caring actions—at home or in the community. Then ask your child to share ways other family members show that they are disciples of Jesus.

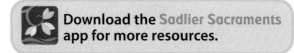

Download the Sadlier Sacraments app for more resources.

Gathering to Give Thanks and Praise

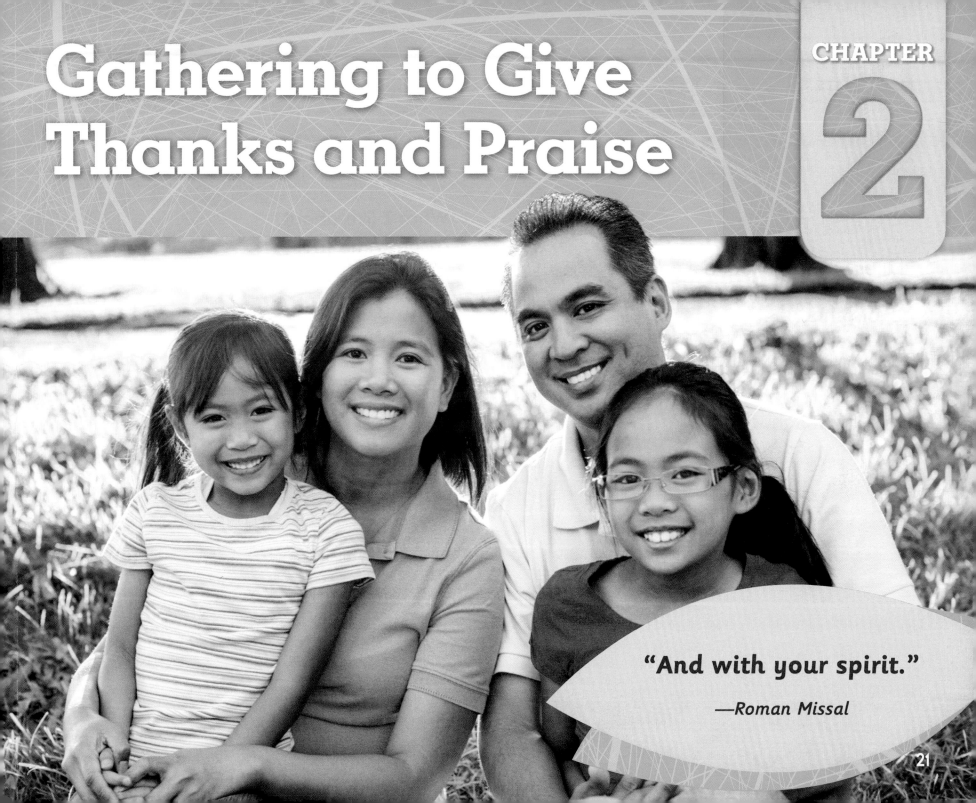

CHAPTER 2

"And with your spirit."

—Roman Missal

Believe

Open Your Heart

Places where I meet new people:

☐ at school

☐ at family gatherings

☐ in my neighborhood

other: _____

_____

_____

What I like about being with others:

_____

_____

_____

_____

Ways new friends help me:

_____

_____

_____

_____

Connecting with Others

Each of us is connected to other people. At school, for example, we gather with other children to learn, share ideas, and make new friends.

How do you feel when you make a new friend? What is the difference between doing things alone and doing things with others?

Through the grace of our Baptism we are connected to Jesus and his Church. When we gather with our parish community at Mass, we share and celebrate our love for God. By the power of the Holy Spirit, Jesus is with the Church as we remember him and give praise and thanks to God.

> "Where two or three are gathered together in my name, there am I in the midst of them."
>
>  MATTHEW 18:20

Believe

The Word of the Lord

Jesus and his disciples often gathered together to celebrate Jewish feasts and holy days. Together they gave praise and thanks to God the Father for his blessings. For some feasts they went to the Temple in Jerusalem to celebrate with other Jewish families. The Temple was the holy place where Jewish People prayed and worshiped God.

 Based on MARK 11:8–9

The week before Jesus died and rose again, he and his disciples went to Jerusalem. Many people were there to celebrate the important Jewish feast of Passover. People heard that Jesus and his disciples were coming to celebrate. Many people went to meet Jesus. Some spread out their coats on the road. Others spread palm tree branches or waved them as Jesus passed. People began to praise Jesus. They called out,

"Hosanna!

Blessed is he who comes in the name of the Lord!"

(Mark 11:9)

Celebrate

People of all ages and backgrounds gather for Mass to worship God.

Gathered for Worship

Every Sunday we gather with our parish to worship God as our Creator and Lord. To **worship** God means to "praise and thank" him. We do this in the greatest prayer of thanksgiving, which we call the Eucharist. This celebration of the Eucharist is also called the Mass. By special words and actions, we show that we believe that God is with us. Most of all, we remember and celebrate how Jesus saved us by his suffering, Death, Resurrection, and Ascension. The community of people who gather for the celebration of the Eucharist is called the **assembly**. Our parish priest leads the assembly in this celebration. He is called the celebrant. A deacon often assists him. At Mass the priest and the deacon wear special clothing called **vestments**.

It was on a Sunday that Jesus Christ rose from the dead to new life. So, Sunday is the most special day for the Church. On Sunday we worship with our parish community, rest from work, and take time to be with our family.

The Church tells us to worship God by taking part in the Mass every Sunday of the year. We are also to attend Mass on other special days called Holy Days of Obligation. When we do this, we follow the Third Commandment and one of the laws of the Church.

Sunday is called the **Lord's Day**. Its celebration lasts from Saturday evening through Sunday until midnight. We gather with our parish to celebrate the Mass on this day because it is the day Jesus rose from the dead. We celebrate the salvation that Jesus made possible by his sacrifice on the Cross. He fills us, the Body of Christ, with the grace of his salvation. The celebration of the Eucharist is the center of the Church's life.

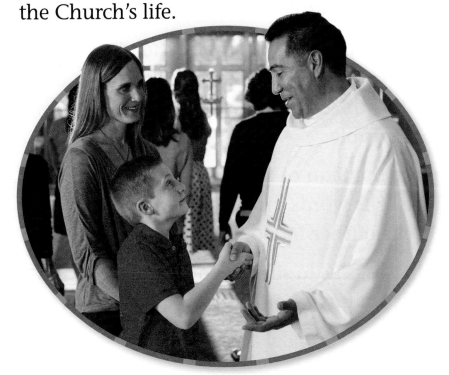

In the celebration of the Eucharist, the Mass, we show God our love by singing, praying, and listening to the Word of God. Together, with the priest, we

- praise and thank God

- listen to the Word of God

- remember Jesus' life, Death, Resurrection, and Ascension

- receive Jesus in Holy Communion.

Celebrate

The Introductory Rites

The Mass begins with the **Introductory Rites**. These prayers and actions help us to remember that we are a worshiping community. They prepare us to listen to the Word of God and celebrate the Eucharist. In the Introductory Rites:

- We stand and sing to express our unity as the baptized. As the assembly sings, the priest, deacon, and other ministers process to the altar.

- Those in the procession bow to the altar or genuflect to the tabernacle, and the priest and deacon kiss the altar as a sign of reverence for the Lord's Table.

- We make the Sign of the Cross. Then the priest greets us. His words and our response remind us that we gather in God's name.

- The priest asks us to silently think about our sins, the times we have not loved God and others.

We begin the Mass by praying through song. This song introduces the liturgical season and feast and expresses our unity.

- Together with the priest we praise God for his love and forgiveness. We may pray:

  "Lord, have mercy."
  "Christ, have mercy."
  "Lord, have mercy."

- We often sing or say a prayer of praise to God the Father, God the Son, and God the Holy Spirit. This prayer begins with the words:

  "Glory to God in the highest,
  and on earth peace to people
  of good will."

- The priest prays an opening prayer to remind us we are in God's presence. We respond, "Amen."

CATHOLIC IDENTITY

"Eucharist . . . is an action of thanksgiving to God."

(*Catechism of the Catholic Church*, 1328)

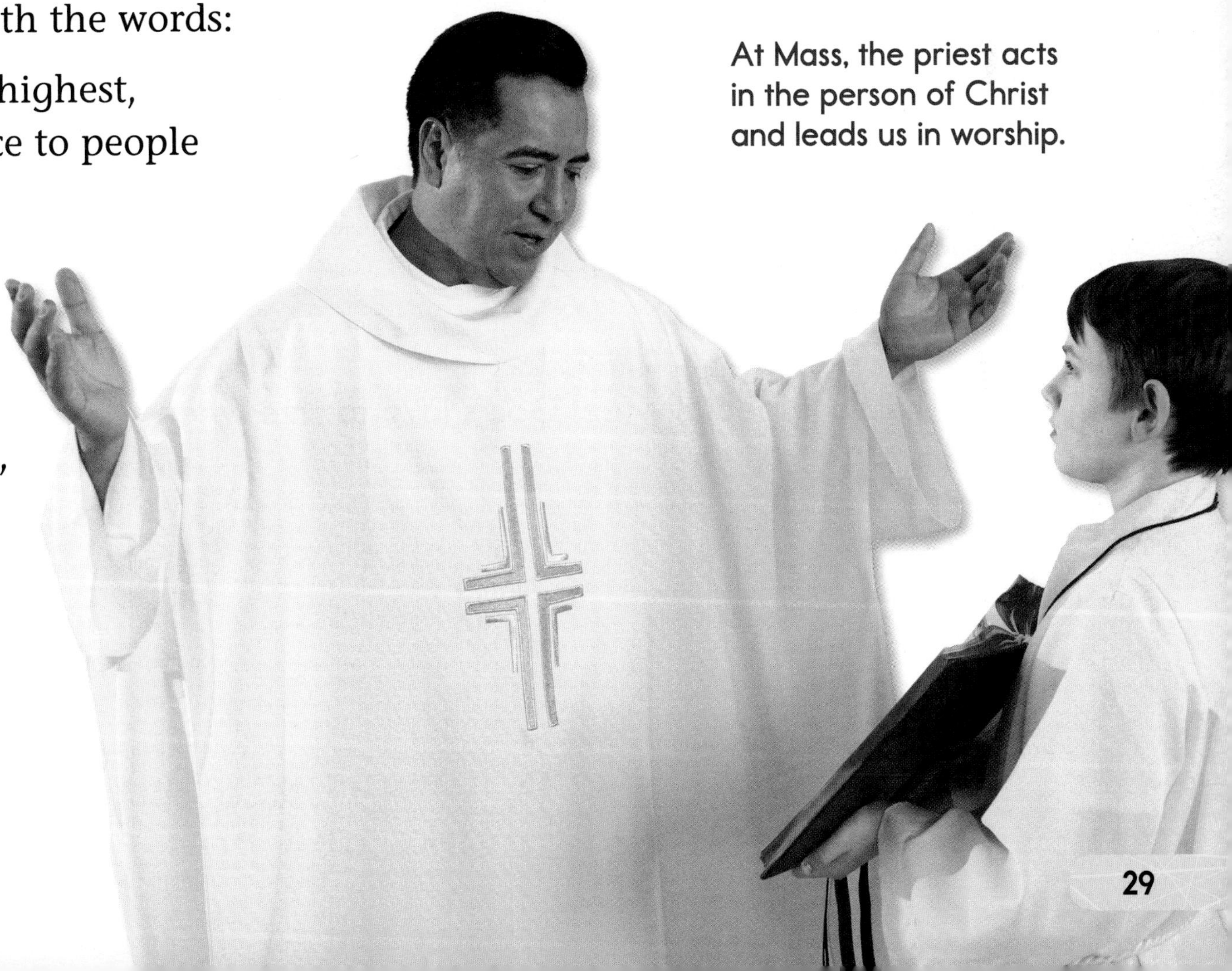

At Mass, the priest acts in the person of Christ and leads us in worship.

Live

Become What You Believe

When my parish community gathers for the celebration of the Mass:

I see . . .

I hear . . .

I pray . . .

At Mass I especially feel God's love for me when . . .

God's love is always with me, and
I give thanks and praise.

Discipleship in Action

Saint Maria Guadalupe (1878–1963)

Saint Maria Guadalupe was born in Mexico. From an early age, she tried to live as a good disciple of Jesus. She prayed often. She was devoted to the Blessed Virgin Mary. Maria also wanted to help people in her community. When she grew up, she decided not to get married. Instead, she became a religious sister to help people in need. Maria founded a new congregation of sisters who served the community. Maria raised money to support the community's hospital. Today the congregation that Maria started serves many poor and sick people in the community.

Here is a drawing of people in the community I can help:

Here is one way I might help them:

_____

_____

Here is a way I will pray for them:

_____

_____

Live

Rain Down Your Love

Leader: Let us make the Sign of the Cross and then sing together "Rain Down."

All: (*Refrain*) Rain down, rain down, rain down your love on your people. Rain down, rain down, rain down your love, God of life.

Leader: God of all creation, we believe that you rain down your love on the earth. Fill us with your mercy as we turn our hearts to you in prayer.

All: (*Sing refrain.*)

Leader: Loving and merciful God, we thank you for the gift of your Son, Jesus. With great joy in our hearts, we give thanks and celebrate with all of our brothers and sisters.

All: (*Sing refrain.*)

Leader: O God, you rain down your Holy Spirit on all who follow you, that we might be your eyes, your hands, and your feet in this world. Thank you for filling us with your love.

All: (*Sing refrain.*)

Leader: We ask God to bless us and those we love, and to help us to remember how much Jesus loves us.

I invite you to take hold of the cross, say a prayer, and then pass the cross on. (*instrumental music*)

All: (*Sing refrain.*)

Leader: Let us join hands and pray as Jesus taught us.

All: Our Father . . .

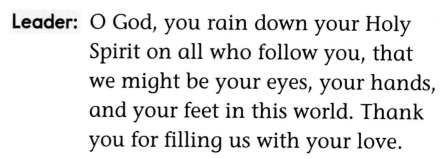

Living Faith at 🏠 Home

"Hosanna! Blessed is he who comes in the name of the Lord!"

MARK 11:9

Take a few minutes to reflect on the Scripture art. Ask God to open your eyes and your heart. What feelings are you experiencing? How do you welcome and honor Jesus with your parish community? Pray a silent prayer of gratitude.

Growing in Fai✝h Together

Help your child to appreciate and treasure the blessings of the Catholic faith. Look at each faith message below. Share from your heart, and listen for the beauty and truth your child holds. Take some quality time together.

On the Lord's Day we worship God with our parish community. We thank God for his love and forgiveness. The celebration of the Eucharist is the heart and center of our Catholic faith.

✝ Pay attention to the ways we show reverence for God at Mass on the Lord's Day, such as by making the Sign of the Cross, by singing, or by our silence. At each Mass, encourage your child to participate more fully in the prayers and actions of the Mass.

The priest is ordained in the Sacrament of Holy Orders. When he celebrates the Eucharist (Mass) or the other sacraments, the priest is acting in the person of Christ.

✝ With your child, name the priests in your parish and discuss their special role in the celebration of the Mass. Have your child close his or her eyes and imagine being at Mass. What are some of the special actions and prayers of the priest that help us to experience that God is really with us?

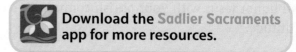

Download the Sadlier Sacraments **app for more resources.**

CHAPTER 3

Celebrating the Liturgy of the Word

"Glory to you, O Lord."

—Roman Missal

Believe

Open Your Heart

Listening is a way to show love. Complete the statements and drawing below.

People I like to listen to include . . .

_____

_____

Places where I listen
to others include . . .

_____

_____

A picture of me listening carefully
to someone:

When God Speaks

There are good reasons why we listen. Listening is a way to learn. It shows that we care. But good listeners do more than hear words. A careful listener also tries to understand what is said and responds in some way.

What is it like when someone listens to you and responds to what you said?

"**Be doers of the word and not hearers only.**"

✝ JAMES 1:22

God invites us to listen to him. At Mass, God speaks to us in the readings we hear from Scripture. These readings help us to understand God better. Like a plant needs water and sunshine to grow, we need the Word of God to grow in faith, hope, and love.

When you hear the Word of God at Mass, listen with attention and an open mind and heart. Know that God is speaking to you. Respond by giving thanks to God for his love. Then go and share the truth of God's love with others.

Believe

The Word of the Lord

One day a large crowd gathered to hear Jesus teach. Jesus told them this story. You can read this story with your friends and family, too.

 Based on MATTHEW 13:3–8, 23

Once a farmer went out to his fields and scattered seeds. Some seeds did not fall in his field. They fell on a path. Birds came and ate these seeds. Some seeds fell on rocky ground. The soil was not very deep. Plants began to grow. But then they dried up and died. Other seeds fell into the thorns and weeds. Plants started to grow. But the thorns and weeds choked these plants.

"But some seed fell on rich soil." (Matthew 13:8) These seeds grew into strong, healthy plants and produced fruit.

Jesus explained the meaning of his story. He said that people who listen carefully to the Word of God are like the seeds in the rich soil. They grow in God's love and share his love with others.

Celebrate

Proclaiming the Word of the Lord

The Bible is the book of the Word of God. It is also called Sacred Scripture. The Bible has two parts, the Old Testament and the New Testament. In the Old Testament we learn about God's people who lived before the time of Jesus. In the New Testament we learn about Jesus and his disciples and about the beginning of the Church. Every Sunday at Mass we listen to three readings from Sacred Scripture. We listen to God speaking to us through his Word. This takes place during the Liturgy of the Word. The **Liturgy of the Word** is the part of the Mass in which we listen to Scripture being proclaimed. To *proclaim* means "to announce."

> The Liturgy of the Word includes these parts:
> - First Reading
> - Responsorial Psalm
> - Second Reading
> - Alleluia or Gospel Acclamation
> - Gospel
> - Homily
> - Profession of Faith (Creed)
> - Prayer of the Faithful

CATHOLIC IDENTITY
The Word of God helps us to grow in faith and love.

We listen carefully to the Word of God. God teaches us how to love him and treat others with kindness.

On most Sundays the first reading is from the Old Testament. From this reading we learn what God did for the Jewish People before Jesus was born. We learn that God's love for his people never ends. The Responsorial Psalm is our response to the first reading. A cantor sings or a reader proclaims the psalm. We sing or say a response. A **psalm** is a song of praise from the Old Testament.

The second reading is from the New Testament. During this reading we listen to the teachings of the Apostles and other disciples. We learn about the beginning of the Church.

The third reading is the **Gospel**. The Gospels are four books of the New Testament that tell about Jesus' life and teachings. The word *gospel* means "good news." On most Sundays we sing *Alleluia* before the Gospel is read. When we listen to the Gospel, we learn the Good News about Jesus Christ and how to live as his disciples.

Throughout the year, as the Church proclaims the readings at Mass, we remember and celebrate the whole mystery of Christ. We celebrate the Incarnation, or the Son of God becoming man, and the Nativity, or the birth of Jesus. We celebrate Jesus' Death, Resurrection, and Ascension, his sending of the Holy Spirit on Pentecost, and his coming again at the end of time.

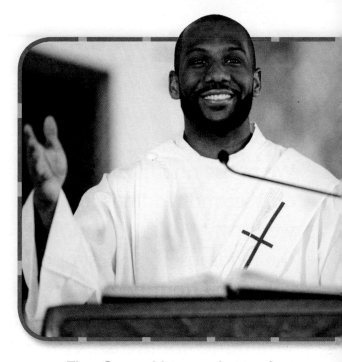

The Gospel has a place of honor in the Liturgy of the Word, so we stand when the priest or deacon proclaims the Gospel.

Celebrate

Responding to the Word of God

We praise and thank God during the Liturgy of the Word. After the first and second readings, we pray, "Thanks be to God." After the Gospel, we pray, "Praise to you, Lord Jesus Christ." After we have heard all the readings, the priest or deacon talks to us about them. This talk is called the **homily**. When we listen carefully to the homily, we learn more about God. We learn ways we can share God's love with others. When the homily is finished, we pray the **Creed**. In the Creed we proclaim the faith of the Church. We believe in God the Father, God the Son, and God the Holy Spirit. We believe in the Church and in God's forgiveness of our sins.

During the Liturgy of the Word, we pray the Creed, a prayer stating what we believe as Catholics.

The parish community listens to the readings from Sacred Scripture.

After the Creed we pray the **Prayer of the Faithful**. In the Prayer of the Faithful, we pray for the needs of the Church. We pray for the pope, other Church leaders, and all God's people. We pray for world leaders. We pray for people throughout the world, especially for those who are sick or in need. We pray for the people in our parish who have died. We pray for people in our lives who need God's love and help. After each prayer, we ask God to hear our prayer.

In the Liturgy of the Word:

- A reader, or **lector**, reads the first two readings. They are read from a book called the **Lectionary**. The lector stands at the **ambo** to read. An ambo is a sacred reading stand, the Table of the Word of God. We sit and listen to the readings.

- A priest or deacon stands at the ambo to read from the Gospel of Matthew, Mark, Luke, or John. The Gospel is most often read from a special book called the **Book of the Gospels**. We stand as the Gospel is read because the Gospel has a place of honor in the Liturgy of the Word.

During the Liturgy of the Word, God speaks to us through Sacred Scripture. Sacred Scripture is proclaimed from the *ambo*, or "Table of the Word of God."

Live

Become What You Believe

I listen to the Word of God at Mass.

What I learn by listening to the Word of God:

_____

_____

_____

_____

_____

Ways I respond to the Word of God:

_____

_____

_____

_____

_____

The Word of God gives me strength.

Discipleship in Action

Saint Benedict (A.D. 480–547)

Saint Benedict was from a wealthy family in the busy city of Rome. As a young adult, he became unhappy with this life and wanted to become holier. So, he left Rome for a quiet place in the mountains. Once there, he lived alone. He devoted himself to strengthening his relationship with God. He read Scripture, prayed, and reflected in silence. After a few years, Benedict was chosen to lead a group of monks. He led the monastic community to seek the glory of God through a life of listening and reflecting on the Word of God.

I listen to the Word of God in my life by . . .

_____

_____

_____

I can share the Word of God with others by . . .

_____

_____

_____

Live

Lord, Hear My Prayer/ Oyenos, Señor

Leader: Let us make the Sign of the Cross and then sing together.

All: (*Refrain*) Lord, hear our prayer. *Oyenos, Señor.* Lord, hear our prayer. *Oyenos, Señor.*

Leader: For the holy Church, that the Lord watch over her and care for her, let us pray to the Lord.

All: (*Sing refrain.*)

Leader: For the peoples of all the world, that the Lord may unite and bless them, let us pray to the Lord.

All: (*Sing refrain.*)

Leader: For all who need care and healing, that the Lord will help them, let us pray to the Lord.

All: (*Sing refrain.*)

Leader: For our families, our friends, our neighbors, and ourselves, that the Lord will hear all of our prayers, let us pray to the Lord.

All: (*Sing refrain.*)

Leader: At this time, I invite you to offer a prayer of your own.

All: (*Sing refrain.*)

Leader: Let us join hands and pray as Jesus taught us.

All: Our Father . . .

Living Faith at Home

"But some seed fell on rich soil."

MATTHEW 13:8

Take a few minutes to reflect on the Scripture art. Ask God to open your eyes and your heart. What feelings are you experiencing? What do you understand from the image about growing? In what ways do you grow? What else do you see? Pray a silent prayer of gratitude.

Growing in Faith Together

Help your child to appreciate and treasure Sacred Scripture and the blessings of the Catholic faith. Look at each faith message below. Share from your heart, and listen for the beauty and truth your child holds. Take some quality time together.

God speaks to us at Mass through Sacred Scripture. During the Liturgy of the Word, we listen to readings from the Old Testament and the New Testament. Through Scripture, we learn more about God and his never-ending love for us.

✠ Share with one another a well-known story from the Old Testament, such as the story of Creation, the Exodus, or Noah and the Great Flood. Talk about the things God did for the people in your chosen Scripture story. Then, share the many ways God blesses your family.

Through Scripture, God teaches us to be loving and caring. At Mass and in our lives, we respond to the Word of God by thanking and praising God. We also respond by following Jesus' example of love and by praying for the needs of others.

✠ After Mass talk about the message of the Gospel and discover one way that you can live out the Word of God as a family.

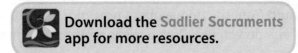

Download the Sadlier Sacraments **app for more resources.**

Celebrating the Liturgy of the Eucharist

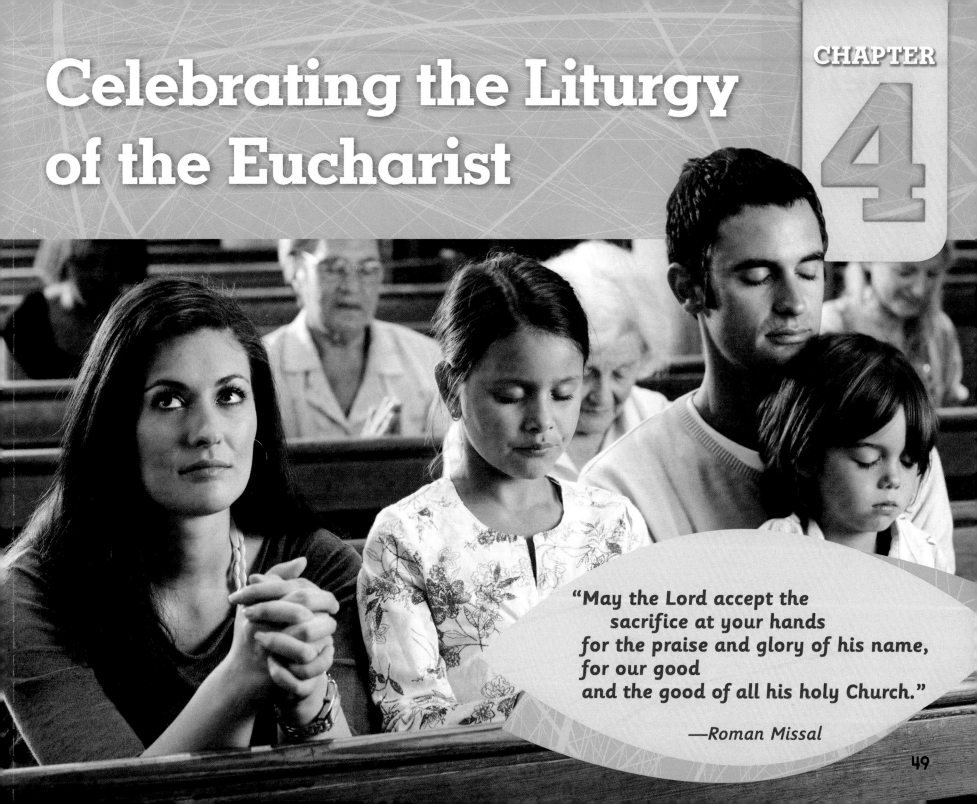

"May the Lord accept the sacrifice at your hands for the praise and glory of his name, for our good and the good of all his holy Church."

—Roman Missal

Believe

Open Your Heart

What are some ways that you give to others?
Name one way in each hand.

A Gift of Love

At what special times does your family give and receive gifts? What is it like for you to give a gift? What is it like to receive a gift?

Giving and receiving gifts is a way to show love. As Catholics, every time we participate in the celebration of the Eucharist we receive the greatest gift of love: the gift of Jesus himself. With joy in our hearts, we give thanks to God for the gift of his Son, Jesus.

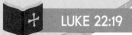

"Do this in memory of me."

LUKE 22:19

 Believe

The Word of the Lord

Passover is an important feast that the Jewish People celebrate every year. During this holy time the Jewish People gather to share a meal and remember that God led their ancestors from slavery to the Promised Land.

 Based on MARK 14:22–24

On the night before Jesus died, he and his disciples, who were Jewish, were getting ready to celebrate the Passover. Here is what Jesus said and did at the meal.

"While they were eating, he took bread, said the blessing, broke it, and gave it to them, and said, 'Take it; this is my body.' Then he took a cup, gave thanks, and gave it to them, and they all drank from it. He said to them, 'This is my blood.'" (Mark 14:22–24)

This was the last meal Jesus shared with his disciples before he died. We call this meal the **Last Supper**. At the Last Supper Jesus gave us the gift of the Eucharist. The Eucharist is the Sacrament of the Body and Blood of Jesus Christ.

Celebrate

The Liturgy of the Eucharist

Jesus told his disciples to remember what he did at the Last Supper. He told them to celebrate this special meal again and again. He said, "Do this in memory of me" (Luke 22:19). Each time we celebrate the Eucharist, we do as Jesus said.

The celebration of the Eucharist is also called the Mass. The word *eucharist* means "to give thanks." Throughout the Mass, we give thanks and praise to God. Like the disciples at the Last Supper, we gather around a table. This special table is called the **altar**. The altar is the focal point of the Liturgy of the Eucharist.

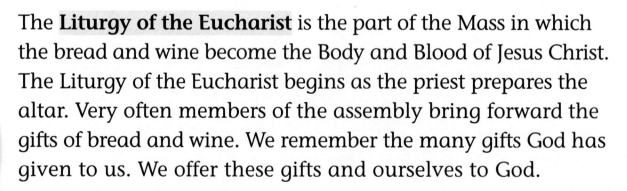

The **Liturgy of the Eucharist** is the part of the Mass in which the bread and wine become the Body and Blood of Jesus Christ. The Liturgy of the Eucharist begins as the priest prepares the altar. Very often members of the assembly bring forward the gifts of bread and wine. We remember the many gifts God has given to us. We offer these gifts and ourselves to God.

We ask the Lord to accept the gifts of bread and wine that we bring to the altar.

The Liturgy of the Eucharist has these parts:

- Preparation of the Gifts
- Prayer over the Offerings
- Eucharistic Prayer
- Communion Rite

The priest or deacon accepts the gifts of bread and wine and places them on the altar. As he prepares the bread and wine, the priest prays special prayers. We respond: *Blessed be God for ever.* Then we pray with the priest that the Lord will accept these gifts.

Throughout the Liturgy of the Eucharist, we remember that the Mass is a sacrifice. A **sacrifice** is an offering of a gift to God. When Jesus was on earth he offered his life for us on the Cross to save us from sin. He rose from the dead on Easter Sunday so that we could live peacefully with God forever. Jesus' work of salvation through his life, Death, and Resurrection is called his Passover. It is remembered and made present in every Mass. And it is Jesus Christ himself who acts through the priest and offers the Eucharistic sacrifice.

Celebrate

The Eucharistic Prayer

After the gifts are prepared, we pray the Eucharistic Prayer. The **Eucharistic Prayer** is the center of the Mass and the Church's greatest prayer of praise and thanksgiving.

The priest prays the Eucharistic Prayer in the name of the whole Church. He prays to God the Father through Jesus Christ in the Holy Spirit. Through the power of the Holy Spirit the priest says and does what Jesus said and did at the Last Supper. Taking the bread the priest says:

> "TAKE THIS, ALL OF YOU, AND EAT OF IT,
>   FOR THIS IS MY BODY,
>   WHICH WILL BE GIVEN UP FOR YOU."

Then taking the cup of wine he says:

> "TAKE THIS, ALL OF YOU, AND DRINK FROM IT,
>   FOR THIS IS THE CHALICE OF MY BLOOD. . . ."

This part of the Eucharistic Prayer is called the **Consecration**.

The priest prays, "FOR THIS IS MY BODY."

The priest prays, "FOR THIS IS THE CHALICE OF MY BLOOD."

During the Liturgy of the Eucharist the priest uses a special plate and cup. The plate is called a **paten**. The priest places the wheat bread that becomes the Body of Christ on the paten. The cup is called a **chalice**. The priest pours the grape wine that becomes the Blood of Christ in the chalice.

By the power of the Holy Spirit and through the words and actions of the priest, the bread and wine become the Body and Blood of Christ. In a way that we cannot fully understand, Jesus Christ is really present in the Eucharist. We call this the **Real Presence**. The changing of the bread and wine into the Body and Blood of Christ is called *transubstantiation*.

Jesus Christ is really present in the Eucharist.

The priest invites us to proclaim our faith. We may pray:

> "When we eat this Bread and drink this Cup, we proclaim your Death, O Lord, until you come again."

We pray that the Holy Spirit will unite all who believe in Jesus. We end the Eucharistic Prayer by praying "Amen." When we do this, we are saying, "Yes, I believe." We are saying "yes" to the prayer the priest has prayed in our name.

Live

Become What You Believe

When we celebrate the Eucharist, we give thanks to God.

THANK YOU

Dear God,

Thank you for the gifts you have given me:

_____

_____

_____

Love,

_____
Name

Jesus is with me!

Discipleship in Action

Saint Brigid (A.D. 453–523)

Saint Brigid was the daughter of an Irish king. From a young age she was known for her kind and giving ways. She would give food and clothing to the poor. She even sometimes gave away things that belonged to her father, the king! When Brigid grew up she became a nun. Saint Brigid started the first religious community of women in Ireland. She helped to build many convents and schools all over Ireland. Saint Brigid was known for sharing peace and kindness with everyone she met.

I can show kindness to someone in need by . . .

Live

Our God Is Here

All: (*Listen to verse one.*)

Here in this time, here in this place, here we are standing face to face. . . .

(*Refrain*) And we cry: "Holy, Holy, Holy are you!"

We cry: "Holy, Holy, Holy and true!"

Amen, we do believe our God is here.

Our God is here.

Leader: God is here with us now, and in a special way in the Body and Blood of Jesus. Each time we go to Mass and receive Holy Communion, we celebrate the love of God in Jesus.

All: (*Listen to verse two.*)

Here in the Word, God is revealed, here where the wounded can be healed. . . .

(*Sing refrain.*)

Leader: Lord Jesus, you are alive in our hearts. Help us to bring your love to our families, and to our friends and neighbors in the world. Help us to be your light in the world. Let us join hands and pray as Jesus taught us.

All: Our Father . . .

Living Faith at ome

Jesus said, "Do this in memory of me."

LUKE 22:19

Take a few minutes to reflect on the Scripture art. Ask God to open your eyes and your heart. What feelings are you experiencing? What does the image teach you about this gathering of Jesus and his disciples? What else do you see? Pray a silent prayer of gratitude.

Growing in Fai✝h Together

Help your child to appreciate and treasure the blessings of the Catholic faith. Look at each faith message below. Share from your heart, and listen for the beauty and truth your child holds. Take some quality time together.

Each Sunday we participate in the celebration of the Eucharist, or the Holy Sacrifice of the Mass. The word *eucharist* means "to give thanks." At Mass we praise God and give him thanks for the gift of our salvation.

✝ When you gather for a family meal, develop the practice of giving thanks to God. During family meals take time to share with each other what happened during the day, especially the things you are thankful for.

At each Mass, by the power of the Holy Spirit, as the priest prays according to the words and actions of Jesus at the Last Supper, the gifts of bread and wine become the Body and Blood of Christ. Jesus Christ is really present.

✝ Spend some time praying before the Blessed Sacrament in the tabernacle at your Church. Always genuflect before the tabernacle to show your reverence for the presence of Christ. Kneel before the tabernacle and take time to talk to God and to listen to him, too. Afterward, discuss your experience.

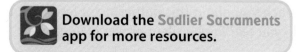

Download the Sadlier Sacraments **app for more resources.**

Receiving the Body and Blood of Christ

CHAPTER 5

"Blessed are those called to the supper of the Lamb."

—Roman Missal

Believe

Open Your Heart

Draw yourself at a celebration with family and friends. On the line, write one word to tell how you feel at the celebration.

A Special Invitation

Celebrations bring people together. Think of your favorite celebrations with family or friends. When we gather with others to celebrate, we share love and joy.

What is it like to be invited to a celebration?

Jesus brought all his disciples together at the Last Supper. Jesus invites us to continue celebrating this sacred meal. At the celebration of the Eucharist we receive Jesus, the Bread of Life. We gather as the Body of Christ. We share love and joy as God's family.

Jesus said, "I am the bread of life."

 JOHN 6:35

Believe

The Word of the Lord

Before he returned to his Father in heaven, the Risen Jesus often visited his disciples.

 Based on LUKE 24:13–35

It was the Sunday that Jesus had risen from the dead. Two of Jesus' disciples were walking to Emmaus, a town near Jerusalem. A man started walking with them. They did not know that this man was the Risen Jesus.

The disciples talked to the man about what had happened the past three days: Jesus was crucified, died, and was buried. And now his body was missing from the tomb.

It was getting dark when they reached the town. The disciples asked the man to stay. He did, and joined them for a meal. Then, "while he was with them at table, he took bread, said the blessing, broke it, and gave it to them" (Luke 24:30).

Then the disciples recognized that this man was the Risen Jesus. They knew him "in the breaking of the bread" (Luke 24:35).

Celebrate

Preparing for Holy Communion

In the Liturgy of the Eucharist, after the Eucharistic Prayer, we prepare to receive Jesus himself in the Eucharist. Through the power of the Holy Spirit and the action of the priest, our gifts of bread and wine have now become the Body and Blood of Christ. And we will receive the Body and Blood of Christ in **Holy Communion**. Like the disciples at Emmaus, we recognize Jesus "in the breaking of the bread."

We join ourselves with the whole Church as we pray aloud or sing the Lord's Prayer. Then the priest reminds us of Jesus' words at the Last Supper. Jesus said, "Peace I leave with you; my peace I give to you" (John 14:27).

We share the gift of Christ's peace with one another.

We pray that Christ's peace may be with us always. We share a **sign of peace** with the people who are near us. When we do this we show that we are united to the Risen Lord, Jesus Christ, and to one another as the Body of Christ.

After we share a sign of peace, we pray to Jesus, who sacrificed his life to save us from sin. We ask him for forgiveness and peace. We begin the prayer with these words:

> "Lamb of God, you take away
> the sins of the world,
> have mercy on us."

As we pray the Lamb of God, the priest breaks the **Host**, the Bread that has become the Body of Christ. The priest puts a small piece in the chalice as a sign of the unity of the Body and Blood of Jesus Christ.

Like Jesus at the Last Supper, the priest breaks the Bread that has become the Body of Christ.

Celebrate

Receiving Holy Communion

After we pray the Lamb of God, the priest invites us to receive Jesus Christ in Holy Communion. The priest prays,

> "Behold the Lamb of God,
> behold him who takes away the sins of the world.
> Blessed are those called to the supper of the Lamb."

Together with the priest we pray,

> "Lord, I am not worthy
> that you should enter under my roof,
> but only say the word
> and my soul shall be healed."

Then we go forward with reverence and love to receive Jesus in Holy Communion. Each of us stands before the priest, deacon, or extraordinary minister of Holy Communion, who raises the Host before us. We bow our head. The priest, deacon, or extraordinary minister says, "The Body of Christ." We respond, "Amen," and then receive the Host in the hand or on the tongue.

We bow our head before receiving the Host, the Body of Christ.

Jesus is offering his very self to us in Holy Communion. When we respond, "Amen," we show that we believe Jesus is really present. We welcome Jesus with open hearts.

We may choose to receive the Host, the Body of Christ, on our tongue.

If we are also receiving from the chalice, the priest, deacon, or extraordinary minister of Holy Communion raises the chalice. Again, we bow our head. The priest, deacon, or extraordinary minister says, "The Blood of Christ." We respond, "Amen," and then drink from the cup.

As the gathered assembly joins in procession and receives the Body and Blood of Christ, we sing a hymn to express our unity. We are united with the whole Church, the Body of Christ.

After everyone has received Holy Communion there is usually some time for quiet prayer. During this time we remember that Jesus is present within us. We thank Jesus for the gift of himself in Holy Communion.

When we drink from the chalice in Holy Communion, we receive the Blood of Christ.

Become What You Believe

Invite someone special to attend Mass. Complete the invitation below.

To: _____

You are invited to _____

Day and time: _____

Place: _____

Prepare for this celebration by _____

_____

_____

_____

_____

I am blessed to be called to the Lord's Supper.

Discipleship in Action

Saint Josephine Bakhita (1869–1957)

As a child, Josephine Bakhita lived as a slave in Sudan, in Africa. Her life was very difficult, but she still saw beauty in the world around her. In her heart, Josephine longed to know God. Eventually she came to live with kind and caring nuns in Italy, where she gained her freedom. The nuns helped Josephine to see God's goodness and love. They taught her to become a follower of Jesus Christ and prepare for Baptism. And they welcomed her when she was called by God to join their religious community. Josephine was a joyful nun. She was happy to help others experience God's love and peace. *Bakhita* means "fortunate one."

I thank God for all the people who help me to follow Jesus Christ, including . . .

Live

Bread of Life/*Pan de Vida*

All: (*Refrain*) *Pan de Vida, cuerpo del Señor,*
cup of blessing, blood of Christ the Lord.
At this table the last shall be first.
Poder es servir, porque Dios es amor.

Leader: We receive the Body of Christ, the Bread of Life.
We drink of the cup of blessing, the Blood of Christ the Lord.

When we receive Holy Communion, we receive the Body of Christ, the Bread of Life. We bring the peace of Christ to those we love and to the world.

All: (*Refrain*)

Leader: This sacred meal that we will share is given to us so that we may share the love of Jesus in the world. We are blessed to be called to the Table of the Lord.

All: (*Refrain*)

Leader: When we eat this bread and drink this cup we proclaim the Death of the Lord, until he comes again.

All: (*Refrain*)

Leader: The peace of the Lord is with us, and we are to share Christ's peace with others. Let us offer one another a sign of peace.

Pan de Vida (82697) Text: John 13:1–15; Galatians 3:28–29; Bob Hurd and Pia Moriarty. Text and music © 1988, Bob Hurd and Pia Moriarty. Published by OCP. All rights reserved.

Living Faith at Home

Jesus "was made known to them in the breaking of the bread."

✝ LUKE 24:35

Take a few minutes to reflect on the Scripture art. Ask God to open your eyes and your heart. What feelings are you experiencing? What are the people doing? Imagine yourself in the scene. What are you thinking? What else do you see? Pray a silent prayer of gratitude.

Copyright © by William H. Sadlier, Inc. All rights reserved.

Growing in Faith Together

Help your child to appreciate and treasure the blessings of the Catholic faith. Look at each faith message below. Share from your heart, and listen for the beauty and truth your child holds. Take some quality time together.

In the Liturgy of the Eucharist, we share a sign of peace. The sign of peace shows that we are a community joined to Jesus Christ and to one another. Together, we hope for peace and forgiveness for ourselves and for the whole world.

✠ At bedtime, share these words of Jesus from the Last Supper: "Peace I leave with you; my peace I give to you." (John 14:27) Together pray for people in your family or community who are in need of God's peace and forgiveness.

As we prepare to receive Jesus in Holy Communion at Mass, we pray the Lord's Prayer together. In Masses throughout the world, the faithful stand to pray this prayer. Praying the Lord's Prayer connects us to the celebration of the Eucharist in a special way.

✠ Pray the Lord's Prayer as a family. Note the statement "Give us this day our daily bread," and make the connection with Holy Communion. At Mass, watch as the priest extends his arms to lead the assembly in the Lord's Prayer. In this gesture, called *orans*, the priest gathers all present and reminds us that in our prayer we are united with God and one another.

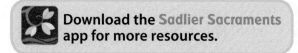
Download the Sadlier Sacraments **app for more resources.**

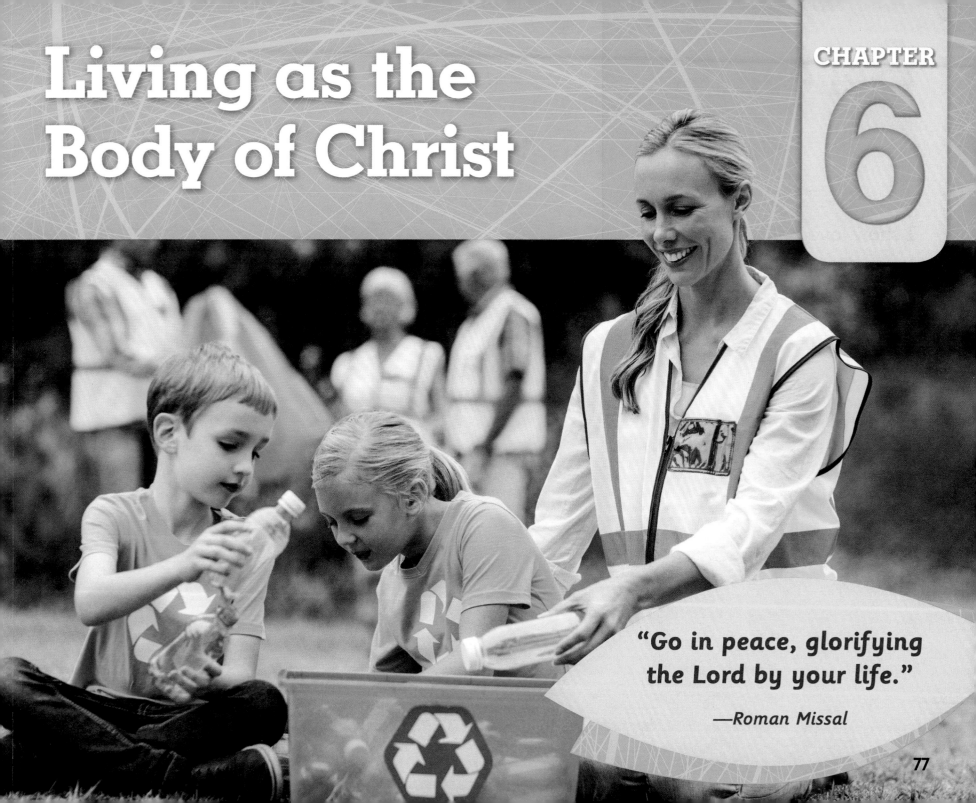

Living as the Body of Christ

CHAPTER

6

"Go in peace, glorifying the Lord by your life."

—Roman Missal

77

Believe

Open Your Heart

I show love and kindness to others . . .

in my words: _____

_____

_____

in my actions: _____

_____

_____

Caring and Helping

Each of us needs the help and care of others. We may need care because we are sick. Maybe we need help with chores or homework. Sometimes we just need someone to show us love and care because we are feeling sad. In the same way, sometimes others need our help and care.

In what ways can I help others in need?

Jesus showed love and care for all people. He comforted and healed those who were sick. He spent time with those who were lonely or rejected. He was patient and forgiving. Jesus calls us to do as he did and help and care for others.

"Love one another as I love you."

JOHN 15:12

79

Believe

The Word of the Lord

After Jesus had risen from the dead, eleven of his disciples gathered on a mountain in Galilee. Jesus had told them to meet him there.

 Based on MATTHEW 28:16–20

When the disciples saw the Risen Christ appear, they could hardly believe their eyes. They worshiped him. Jesus said to them, "All power in heaven and on earth has been given to me. Go, therefore, and make disciples of all nations, baptizing them in the name of the Father, and of the Son, and of the holy Spirit" (Matthew 28:18–19).

Jesus wanted his disciples to share God's love with all people. Jesus wanted his disciples to teach others how to be his followers and friends. Jesus promised his disciples that he would always be with them. He said, "I am with you always" (Matthew 28:20).

Celebrate

Concluding Rites

Jesus sent his disciples out to continue his work. We are disciples of Jesus. He wants us to keep doing his work, too. He wants us to share God's love with others in our homes, schools, parishes, neighborhoods, cities or towns, and throughout the world. God's grace helps us to do all that he asks. We are reminded of this call at Mass.

The celebration of the Mass ends with the **Concluding Rites**, which include a greeting and blessing, dismissal, and reverence of the altar. At the end of Mass, together with the priest, we ask the Lord to be with us. Then the priest gives us a blessing. This final **blessing** is a prayer asking God to keep us in his care. The priest blesses us with the Sign of the Cross as he says,

"May almighty God bless you,
the Father, and the Son, † and the Holy Spirit."

We respond, "Amen."

At the end of Mass, we make the Sign of the Cross as the priest blesses us in God's name.

Then the priest or deacon dismisses us, or sends us out, as baptized members of the Church, to share God's love with others. He says one of the following:

- "Go in peace."

- "Go forth, the Mass is ended."

- "Go and announce the Gospel of the Lord."

- "Go in peace, glorifying the Lord by your life."

We respond, "Thanks be to God."

After the dismissal, sometimes we sing a hymn. During this hymn, the priest, deacon, and other ministers process out of the church. All through the week we remember Jesus' promise to be with us always.

The word *Mass* comes from a word meaning "dismissal," or "to send out." We are sent out as the baptized to follow Jesus' example of love and service.

CATHOLIC IDENTITY
As disciples of Jesus, we love God above all things, and we love our neighbor as ourselves.

83

Celebrate

Continuing Jesus' Work

Every Sunday we are joined to Jesus and the whole Church in the Sacrament of the Eucharist. We receive Jesus in Holy Communion. Our friendship with Jesus grows. Our venial sins are forgiven and we are helped to stay away from serious sin.

Through the Holy Spirit, Jesus is with us as we continue his work. Receiving Jesus in Holy Communion helps us to love God and others. Holy Communion helps us to become stronger disciples of Jesus. It helps us to join our parish community in loving and serving God and others. We are joined more closely to Christ. This makes the unity of the whole Church stronger. Together we are the Mystical Body of Christ.

As disciples of Jesus Christ we can love and serve God and others in many ways. Here are a few of those ways.

- Help out at home or in school.

- Do something kind for a friend or neighbor.

- Give to a food or clothing drive.

- Send a get-well card or make a visit to someone who is sick.

- Pray for others, and especially people who are poor or hungry.

- Forgive others or ask for their forgiveness.

*At Mass, after Holy Communion, there may be consecrated Hosts that have not been received. These Hosts are placed in reserve in the **tabernacle** to bring to the sick and for the adoration of the faithful. The **Most Blessed Sacrament** is another name for the Eucharist. We can visit the church and pray to Jesus, who is present in the Most Blessed Sacrament. We can ask Jesus to help us love and care for others.*

We are disciples of Jesus. When we receive Jesus in Holy Communion we grow in our love for God and others.

Live

Become What You Believe

Complete the statement by drawing yourself in the scene.

Jesus calls me, and I respond by . . .

**As a disciple I am sent out to love
and serve God and others.**

Discipleship in Action

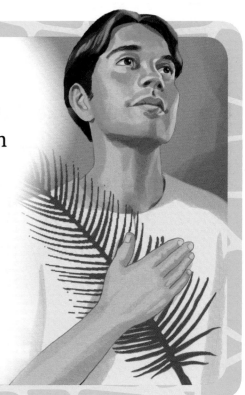

Saint Pedro Calungsod (1654–1672)

Pedro Calungsod grew up in the Philippines in the 1600s. Pedro learned the Catholic faith at school and was a faithful Christian as a child. By the time he was a teenager Pedro was already a catechist. A catechist is a person who teaches others about God and how to live as Jesus did. When Pedro was fourteen, he became a missionary in Guam, an island where people did not know about God. There he spread the Good News of Jesus' love for all people. Through Pedro's teaching and example, many people became followers of Jesus and were baptized.

I can help others know about Jesus' love by . . .

Live

We Are the Body of Christ/
Somos el Cuerpo de Cristo

Leader: Let us make the Sign of the Cross and then sing together.

All: *(Refrain) Somos el cuerpo de Cristo.* We are the body of Christ.

Hemos oído el llamado; we've answered "Yes" to the call of the Lord.

Somos el cuerpo de Cristo. We are the body of Christ.

Traemos su santo mensaje. We come to bring the good news to the world.

(After each verse, sing: We are the body of Christ.)

Bringing the light of God's mercy to others *(Sing)*

Serving each other we build up the kingdom. *(Sing)*

All are invited to feast in the banquet. *(Sing)*

(Sing refrain.)

Leader: Christ lives in us through Baptism, so come forward now to make the Sign of the Cross on your forehead, lips, and heart with the holy water.

All: *(Sing refrain.)*

Leader: Let us offer a sign of peace and pray as Jesus taught us.

All: Our Father . . .

Living Faith at ome

Jesus said, "I am with you always."

MATTHEW 28:20

Take a few minutes to reflect on the Scripture art. Ask God to open your eyes and your heart. What feelings are you experiencing? What do you think it was like to hear Jesus speak in person? What is Jesus saying to you right now? Pray a silent prayer of gratitude.

Growing in Faith Together

Help your child to appreciate and treasure the blessings of the Catholic faith. Look at each faith message below. Share from your heart, and listen for the beauty and truth your child holds. Take some quality time together.

In the Concluding Rites at Mass, the priest or deacon may say, "Go in peace, glorifying the Lord by your life." The assembly is dismissed, or sent out to tell others about Jesus. As baptized members of the Church we are called to spread God's love to others by the way we live and by what we say and do.

 Talk to your child about the people who taught you about Jesus. Then listen as your child tells you about family members, priests, catechists, or other special people who have shared God's love with him or her.

We receive Jesus in Holy Communion. Through the Holy Spirit, Jesus is with us, helping us to live as his disciples. Jesus helps us to love God and others in our homes, schools, parishes, neighborhoods, and cities or towns, and throughout the world.

 Think about the special talents you and your child have. Explore ways to share these talents with others at your home, school, work, or parish. To get started, talk about a kind act someone did for you this week and how it made you feel. Invite your child to do the same. Then together think of a kind act you can do for members of your family or someone in your community in need of help.

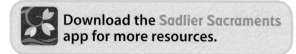
Download the Sadlier Sacraments **app for more resources.**

How to Receive Jesus in Holy Communion

When I receive the Body of Christ in Holy Communion, this is what I do:

I process to the altar with hands joined in prayer.

I sing the communion hymn or chant with the assembly.

When my turn comes, the priest, deacon, or extraordinary minister of Holy Communion raises the Host, and I bow my head.

When I hear the words, "The Body of Christ," I respond, "Amen." I can choose to receive the Host in my hand or on my tongue.

If I choose to receive the Host in my hand, I place my left hand on top of my right hand (or the opposite if I am left-handed). After the Host is placed in my hand, I eat it right away, fold my hands in prayer, and return to my seat.

If I choose to receive the Host on my tongue, I hold my head up and gently put out my tongue. After the Host is placed on my tongue, I swallow it right away, and return to my seat.

I bow my head.

I receive the Host in my hand.

I receive the Host on my tongue.

91

If I am going to receive from the chalice, I first swallow the Host. I walk to the priest, deacon, or extraordinary minister of Holy Communion holding the chalice.

The chalice is raised before me, and I bow my head.

When I hear the words "The Blood of Christ," I respond, "Amen." Then I take a sip from the chalice. After I receive from the chalice, I fold my hands in prayer and return to my seat.

After I receive Communion, this is what I do:

I sing the Communion chant, or song, with my parish family.

Once the chant or song is completed, I spend time in quiet prayer.

I receive from the chalice.

Eucharistic Fast

As a sign of respect and reverence for Jesus in the Eucharist, we must have not taken any food or drink for one hour before receiving Holy Communion. This is called the Eucharistic fast. Water and medicine may be taken during the Eucharistic fast.

Leading a Sacramental Life

Receive Holy Communion often and the Sacrament of Penance and Reconciliation regularly. Follow the laws of the Church, which say: We must attend Mass on Sundays and other Holy Days of Obligation. We must receive Holy Communion once a year, at least during the Easter season. We must confess our sins once a year if we have committed mortal, or serious, sin.

When we receive Holy Communion, we must always be in the state of grace. Anyone who has committed a mortal sin must receive absolution in the Sacrament of Penance and Reconciliation before receiving Holy Communion.

Lord's Prayer

Our Father, who art in heaven,
hallowed be thy name;
thy kingdom come;
thy will be done on earth
    as it is in heaven.
Give us this day our daily bread;
and forgive us our trespasses
as we forgive those
    who trespass against us;
and lead us not into temptation,
but deliver us from evil.
Amen.

Apostles' Creed

I believe in God, the Father almighty,
Creator of heaven and earth,
and in Jesus Christ, his only Son, our Lord,
who was conceived by the Holy Spirit,
born of the Virgin Mary,
suffered under Pontius Pilate,
was crucified, died and was buried;
he descended into hell;
on the third day he rose again from
    the dead;
he ascended into heaven,
and is seated at the right hand
    of God the Father almighty;
from there he will come to judge
    the living and the dead.

I believe in the Holy Spirit,
    the holy catholic Church,
    the communion of saints,
    the forgiveness of sins,
    the resurrection of the body,
    and life everlasting.
Amen.

Prayer before Communion

Jesus, you are the Bread of Life.
Thank you for sharing your life with me.
Help me always to be your friend
    and disciple.

Jesus, help me to welcome you into
    my heart.
Help me to be true to you always.

Prayer after Communion

Jesus, you do such great things for me!
You fill me with your life.
Help me to grow in loving you and
    others.

Jesus, thank you for coming to me in
    Holy Communion.
I love you very much. You come to live
    within me.
You fill me with your life.
Help me to be and do all that you wish.

Prayer before the Most Blessed Sacrament

Jesus,
you are God-with-us,
especially in this Sacrament of
    the Eucharist.
You love me as I am and help me grow.

Come and be with me
in all my joys and sorrows.
Help me share your peace and love
with everyone I meet.
I ask in your name.
Amen.

actual grace (page 14) grace at work in our daily lives, helping us to do good

altar (page 54) the special table that is the center of the celebration of the Liturgy of the Eucharist, also called the Table of the Lord

ambo (page 43) a sacred reading stand called the Table of the Word of God. The ambo is used for the proclamation of Scripture in the liturgy.

assembly (page 26) the community of people who join together for the celebration of the Eucharist or other sacraments

Blessed Trinity (page 12) the Three Persons in One God: God the Father, God the Son, and God the Holy Spirit

blessing (page 82) the prayer that the priest prays over the assembly at the end of Mass, blessing us with the Sign of the Cross and asking God to keep us in his care

Book of the Gospels (page 43) a special book that contains the Gospels of Matthew, Mark, Luke, and John

chalice (page 57) the special cup into which the priest pours the grape wine that becomes the Blood of Christ during the Liturgy of the Eucharist

Church (page 12) the community of people who are baptized and are called to follow Jesus Christ

Concluding Rites (page 82) the last part of the Mass, which includes a greeting and blessing, dismissal, and reverence of the altar

Consecration (page 56) the part of the Eucharistic Prayer when, by the power of the Holy Spirit and through the words and actions of the priest, the bread and wine become the Body and Blood of Christ

Creed (page 42) the prayer in which we proclaim the faith of the Church

Eucharistic Prayer (page 56) the center of the Mass and the Church's greatest prayer of praise and thanksgiving

Gospel (page 41) the Good News about Jesus Christ and how to live as his disciples. The Gospels are four books of the New Testament that tell about Jesus' life and teachings.

Holy Communion (page 68) the receiving of the bread and wine that have become the Body and Blood of Christ at Mass

homily (page 42) the talk given by the priest or deacon at Mass that helps us understand the readings

Host (page 69) the Bread that has become the Body of Christ

Introductory Rites (page 28) the first part of the Mass; prayers and actions that prepare us to listen to the Word of God and celebrate the Eucharist

GLOSSARY

Last Supper (page 52) the last meal Jesus shared with his disciples, on the night before he died

Lectionary (page 43) a special book from which the first two readings of the Mass are read

lector (page 43) a reader who reads the Scripture readings at Mass except for the Gospel

Liturgy of the Eucharist (page 54) the part of the Mass in which the bread and wine become the Body and Blood of Jesus Christ

Liturgy of the Word (page 40) the part of the Mass in which we listen to God's Word being proclaimed

Lord's Day (page 27) Sunday is called the Lord's Day. Its celebration is from Saturday evening through Sunday until midnight.

Mass (page 13) the celebration of the Eucharist

Most Blessed Sacrament (page 85) another name for the Eucharist, the consecrated Hosts

paten (page 57) the special plate on which the priest places the wheat bread that becomes the Body of Christ during the Liturgy of the Eucharist

Prayer of the Faithful (page 43) the prayer after the Creed during the Liturgy of the Word in which we pray for the needs of all God's people

psalm (page 41) a song of praise from the Old Testament

Real Presence (page 57) Jesus Christ being truly present in the Eucharist

sacraments (page 14) special signs given to us by Jesus through which we share in God's life and love

sacrifice (page 55) an offering of a gift to God

sanctifying grace (page 14) the gift of grace that we receive in the sacraments that helps us to respond to God's love and live as Jesus did

sign of peace (page 69) at Mass, a sign that we share with the people who are near us to show that we are united to Christ and to one another

tabernacle (page 85) the special place in the church in which the Most Blessed Sacrament is placed in reserve

vestments (page 26) the special clothing that priests and deacons wear to celebrate Mass or other rites

worship (page 26) to give God thanks and praise